Engineering
Feats & Failures

Stephanie Paris

Consultants

Timothy Rasinski, Ph.D.
Kent State University

Lori Oczkus
Literacy Consultant

John Ferguson, AIA
Architect

Based on writing from
TIME For Kids. *TIME For Kids* and the *TIME For Kids* logo are registered trademarks of TIME Inc. Used under license.

Publishing Credits

Dona Herweck Rice, *Editor-in-Chief*
Lee Aucoin, *Creative Director*
Jamey Acosta, *Senior Editor*
Lexa Hoang, *Designer*
Stephanie Reid, *Photo Editor*
Rane Anderson, *Contributing Author*
Rachelle Cracchiolo, *M.S.Ed., Publisher*

Image Credits: cover, pp.1, 32–33, 38 (bottom), 41 (left & right) NASA; pp.9 (top) 26 (bottom) Alamy; p.27 (bottom) Associated Press; p.40 (left) Bridgeman Art; p.26–27 Bettmann/Corbis; pp.11 (top), 15 (top), 19 (bottom) Getty Images; p.12 (background) duncan1890/iStockphoto; pp.12–13, 24–25, 35 Janelle Bell-Martin; p.40 (right) Emory Kristof/ National Geographic Stock; pp.18–19, 20 (bottom) akg-images/Newscom; pp.29 (top right), 34 (bottom) EPA/Newscom; pp.20–21, 41 (top) picture-alliance/Judaica-Samml/ Newscom; p.29 (bottom left) REUTERS/ Newscom; p.14–15 North Wind Picture Archives; All other images from Shutterstock.

Teacher Created Materials

5301 Oceanus Drive
Huntington Beach, CA 92649-1030
http://www.tcmpub.com
ISBN 978-1-4333-4871-6
© 2013 Teacher Created Materials, Inc.

Table of Contents

Making It Work

Scientists learn things. But **engineers** do things. Engineers use science and math to make things. Sometimes, they solve a big problem. They may find a way to build a bridge across a river. Other times, they make life easier. It was an engineer who figured out how to make water flow from a sink.

For thousands of years, engineers have made huge buildings. They have created great machines. Again and again, they find brilliant ways to solve problems. But engineers are people. And people make mistakes. Sometimes, the most amazing **feats** turn into terrible failures.

THINK LINK

- How is new technology developed?
- Why are failures and mistakes big parts of success?
- How have advances in science, technology, and engineering improved our lives?

Early Engineers

Ancient engineers made huge structures with basic tools. They used ramps, levers, and simple rollers. These tools helped them build monuments that still impress people today. People are still trying to figure out how these ancient engineers did their work!

The Great Pyramid of Giza

Because they were built so long ago, few ancient feats can still be seen today. But there are some. The Great Pyramid is the only Ancient Wonder of the World that still exists. It was built as a tomb for **Pharaoh** Khufu. It is nearly 450 feet high. Each side measures 756 feet long. It is made from over two million blocks of stone. Each block weighs over two tons! Scientists think workers built large wooden ramps. Then, they dragged each block into place.

There are seven official Ancient Wonders of the World, including gardens, monuments, temples, and a great lighthouse. All the ancient wonders were built between 2650 BC and 280 BC.

Pyramid Workers

Egyptian records show that many of the pyramid workers were forced to work. But they were treated well by the standards of the time. There were rules about how many hours they could work each day. They had fair **wages**, and there were even official holidays.

Monument Math

If the Great Pyramid has 2,300,000 stones and each stone weighs 2.5 tons, how heavy is the Great Pyramid?

2.5 tons x 2,300,000 stones = ?

The Great Wall

Ancient Chinese rulers had a problem. They needed a better way to stop invaders. So they built a wall nearly 25 feet tall and 2,000 miles long. The wall wasn't built overnight. It took close to 1,800 years to complete.

The wall was made in **segments**. The segments were connected over many years. Together, they form the giant wall that exists today. **Passes** allowed people to travel from one side of the wall to the other. Soldiers watched for danger from **signal towers**.

Engineers used rivers, lakes, and mountains to extend the wall. With these natural dividers, the wall protects over 5,500 miles.

The Great Failure

Even though the Great Wall is the longest wall in the world, eventually it failed to keep out invaders. Genghis Khan (GANG-gus KAHN), a Mongol ruler, and his army were a threat to China. In part, the wall was built to stop them, but they found a way around it. Kahn and his army **conquered** most of China in AD 1211.

Stonehenge

Around 2,950 BC, engineers began building. Over 1,000 years later, they completed a ring of huge stones. It's thought that Stonehenge took over 20 million hours to create. But none of us know for sure why it was built!

Some of the stones came from nearly 200 miles away. How did the workers move these four-ton stones without modern tools? The wheel hadn't been invented yet. Some scientists think the stones were dragged in giant baskets. Others think pebbles were used to roll them.

Ancient Failures

Many people have seen the Leaning Tower of Pisa. It was built in AD 1173. But engineers made a mistake. They built on soft ground. One side of the tower sank into the ground. But the tower did not fall. Early builders certainly had many mistakes and failures like this.

What problem do you think ancient engineers were trying to solve with this stone monument?

DIG DEEPER!

Seven Wonders of the Ancient World

They aren't called the Seven Wonders of the Ancient world for nothing! All but one were destroyed over 1,000 years ago. But the world still remembers them.

The Hanging Gardens of Babylon were built around 600 BC in what is now Iraq. They were destroyed by an earthquake in 226 BC.

The Great Pyramid was built around 2750 BC in Giza, Egypt as a tomb for the pharaoh. This massive stone structure is nearly 450 feet high. It still exists.

Known for its beauty, the Temple of Artemis at Ephesus was built in 550 BC in what is now modern-day Turkey. It was destroyed by a raid in AD 262.

Built in 435 BC, the Statue of Zeus at Olympia stood over 40 feet tall. It was coated in gold and ivory. It was destroyed by a fire in AD 462.

The Colossus of Rhodes was a bronze-and-gold statue of the sun god Helios. It was built from 294–282 BC on the Greek island of Rhodes. It was destroyed by an earthquake in 226 BC.

Made of gleaming white marble, the Mausoleum at Halicarnassus stood at 140 feet tall. It was built around 350 BC as a tomb for King Mausolus. It was damaged by earthquakes and then destroyed by the Crusaders in AD 1522.

Built in 280 BC, the Lighthouse of Alexandria was the first of its kind. It guided ships into the harbor in Alexandria, Egypt for more than 1,500 years.

The
Industrial
Age

How can we make things faster? How can we make more? Engineers often try to answer these types of questions. In the 1700s, people learned how to make new kinds of machines. And they made a lot of them. These machines helped engineers build even more complicated machines. The **Industrial Revolution** changed the world. But with great growth, there may be great disaster!

The Transcontinental Railroad

On May 10, 1869, there was a big party in Utah. The rails of the Union Pacific Railroad had just been connected with the Central Pacific Railroad. Two thousand miles of rail connected California to the Missouri River. The trains crossed the dangerous Sierra Nevada mountain range. They went through harsh deserts. The trip used to take four to six months. Now it took six days! This was the world's first **transcontinental** railroad. And it was one of America's greatest engineering feats.

Industrial Disasters

Mining disasters were terribly common in the late 1800s. Sometimes, there was a gas or dynamite explosion. Other times, the miners were buried alive or drowned when a tunnel collapsed. The death tolls were high. Today, mining is still a dangerous job, but there are not as many accidents as there were during the Industrial Age.

Transcontinental means crossing a continent. The First Transcontinental Railroad did not cross all of North America. But the connection let people get from the East Coast to the West Coast.

The Panama Canal

People wanted a faster way to travel around the world. So they built a shortcut. The Panama **Canal** is a man-made river. It was made between 1880 and 1914. It linked the Pacific and Atlantic Oceans. The canal let ships travel around the world much faster. Before, ships had to sail around South America. Now, they could cross the canal.

The engineers had a difficult plan. It required thousands of men to dig the large canal. The workers used **explosives**. Drills and **steam shovels** broke up the earth. The Panama Canal Railway removed the dirt they dug up. The canal needed to be large enough for huge ships to pass through.

The work was dangerous. Builders used dynamite and worked in high places. Deadly diseases made thousands ill. Almost 30,000 workers died building the canal. Today, more than 14,000 ships pass through each year. But every year, workers must repair the canal so ships can continue to pass through.

Windy Wipeout

The Tacoma Narrows Bridge became famous during construction for a bounce workers felt when there were strong winds. They nicknamed it Galloping Gertie. Only four months after its opening, the winds were so strong that the bridge twisted apart and fell into the river below. Then, it became known as "the most dramatic failure in bridge engineering history." Fortunately, no humans died, but a black cocker spaniel named Tubby did.

Atlantic Ocean

The Panama Canal

50 miles

Ships wait to pass through the canal.

Pacific Ocean

Ships had to travel around South Africa before the canal.

The *Titanic* Disaster

On April 10, 1912, the *Titanic* set sail. There were 2,224 people on board. She was the largest luxury ship on the seas. Engineers tried to make her the safest, too. The ship was made to be unsinkable. The lower part of the ship was split into 16 watertight areas. Each one could be sealed off. This meant that if one part had a hole, water wouldn't get into other sections.

But on April 14, 1912, the *Titanic* struck an iceberg. The sharp ice didn't simply make a hole. It ripped a long gash down the side of the ship. It was impossible to seal off the flooding. The ship sank in icy water. Only 710 people survived.

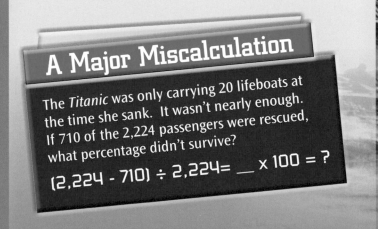

A Major Miscalculation

The *Titanic* was only carrying 20 lifeboats at the time she sank. It wasn't nearly enough. If 710 of the 2,224 passengers were rescued, what percentage didn't survive?

$$(2{,}224 - 710) \div 2{,}224 = \underline{} \times 100 = \,?$$

Most of the people on the *v* died from freezing in the icy water.

A Simple Fix

The *Titanic* had two men assigned to watch for ice. It would have been appropriate at the time for them to use binoculars. But they only used their eyes. By the time the men spotted the iceberg in the water, it was too late to turn the ship. If they had seen it even a little sooner, the disaster may have been avoided!

The *Hindenburg*

In the early 1900s, airships were popular. These were similar to the modern-day **blimp**. They had wooden frames covered in cloth. Inside, **hydrogen** gas made them float. But hydrogen is very **flammable**.

In May 1937, the *Hindenburg* was trying to dock in New Jersey. As it prepared to land, the gas caught fire. Within seconds, the entire ship was in flames! It fell from the sky. There were 97 people on board. Thirty-six were killed in the fiery crash. After this terrible accident, many people didn't want to ride on airships anymore.

Crash and Burn

Airships were designed to let people fly. They quickly proved to be expensive, slow, and dangerous. Airships caused more problems than they solved!

The Smart Choice

The *Hindenburg* disaster made engineers rethink their choice of gases. Today, airships use **helium** instead of hydrogen. Helium won't easily burn or explode. It is a much safer gas.

Hoover Dam

In the early 1900s, engineers had two problems. The Colorado River kept flooding. At the same time, California didn't have enough water. A **dam** could solve both problems.

Most of the Hoover Dam was built during the **Great Depression**. That meant the project helped with one more problem. Over 7,000 people got jobs working on the dam. But there was a high cost. Over 100 people were killed.

Miles of deep tunnels were built to direct the water. Each tunnel was lined with concrete. Inside the tunnels, it was very hot. At times, it was over 120°F. This made for difficult and dangerous work.

Today, the dam is still impressive. It is 726 feet tall and 1,244 feet long. There's enough concrete to build a sidewalk around the world! The water it holds back forms a huge lake.

How Much Water?

The water held back by the dam forms Lake Mead. This lake can hold 1.25 trillion cubic feet of water. That's enough to cover the state of Pennsylvania in a foot of water!

Naming Controversy

Dams were often named for presidents. So, naming the dam after the president who had championed it made sense. But Herbert Hoover was a very unpopular president. Many people blamed him for the Great Depression. For a while, the dam was called the Boulder Dam. But the name didn't catch on. In 1947, the government officially renamed it Hoover Dam. This time, the name stuck.

Inside Hoover Dam

The engineers of the Hoover Dam created one of the largest man-made lakes in the world. Their work prevents flooding, stores water, creates electricity, and connects the Southwest.

More than three miles of tunnels 50 feet in diameter were built as the dam was constructed.

5,000

+

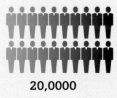

20,0000

Before the construction of the Hoover Dam, only 5,000 people lived in Las Vegas. But the construction of the dam brought 20,000 more.

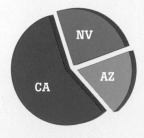

The state of California uses about 56 percent of the power created by the dam's powerhouse. Nevada uses 25 percent. Arizona uses 19 percent.

In 1941 and 1983 the spillways were used during floods.

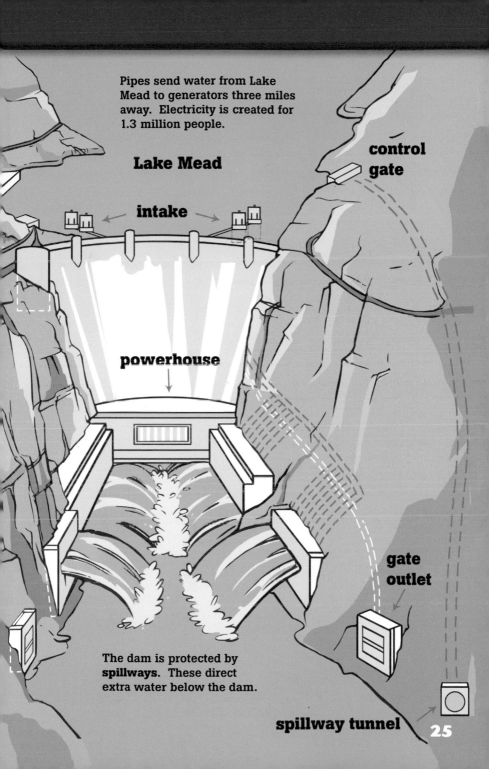

Pipes send water from Lake Mead to generators three miles away. Electricity is created for 1.3 million people.

Lake Mead

intake

control gate

powerhouse

gate outlet

The dam is protected by **spillways**. These direct extra water below the dam.

spillway tunnel

St. Francis Dam Collapse

Hoover Dam was a feat of engineering. But not every dam is a success. Just before midnight on March 12, 1928, there was a scary sound. A 78-foot wall of water roared through California. The St. Francis Dam near Los Angeles had collapsed. Only hours earlier, its chief engineer had inspected it. Out of the dam rushed 12.5 billion gallons of water. It traveled 54 miles to the ocean. The city of Santa Paula was buried under 20 feet of mud. Some places were covered in 70 feet of mud. More than 450 people were killed.

A Terrible Legacy

The chief engineer for the St. Francis Dam was William Mulholland. He worked his way up as a water engineer. He worked on the Panama Canal and even helped plan the Hoover Dam. After the St. Francis Dam's collapse, he was so sad that he stopped working. Although he worked on many successful projects, he is remembered for this huge failure.

A Sticky Mess!

In 1919, a huge tank of **molasses** burst. Over two million gallons flooded Commercial Street in Boston. The 15-foot wave lifted a train right off its tracks! Over 20 people were killed and 150 were injured.

27

Engineering Today

Today, our world is changing quickly. There are many new problems to solve. But today's engineers also have new tools to do their work. These tools let them tackle difficult challenges. **Computer-aided engineering** (CAE) programs make models of machines. They help people understand the products they are designing. With these tools, they can predict how the pieces will fit together. Engineers today can also learn from the feats and failures of the past. In this way, they are solving more problems than ever.

CAE lets engineers see what a car will look like once it is produced.

Taller, Faster, Stronger

Check out some of the biggest and boldest structures in the world—at least until the next one comes along.

The Channel Tunnel is the longest underwater tunnel in the world. It stretches under the English Channel between France and England.

The Gerkin building in London uses 50 percent less energy than similar office buildings.

Abu Dhabi is home to the world's fastest roller coaster.

At 2,700 feet, the Burj Khalifa in Dubai is the tallest structure in the world.

Crunching the Data

The greatest engineering feats took time, money, and thousands of lives to complete. Compare the figures to see what went into and came out of these structures.

	Number of Workers	Time to Complete	
The Transcontinental Railroad	10,000–20,000	$6\frac{1}{2}$ years	
The Panama Canal	40,000	33 years	
The Hoover Dam	10,000–20,000	5 years	

"This morning I came, I saw, and I was conquered as everyone would be who sees for the first time this great feat of mankind."

—President Franklin D. Roosevelt, describing the Hoover Dam

Cost	Number of Deaths	Dimensions	Importance
$50 million	50–150	nearly 1,800 miles long	cut travel time between California and the Missouri River from several months to six days
over $600 million	roughly 27,000	nearly 50 miles long	cut travel time around South America from 10 months to 2 weeks
$49 million	roughly 100	nearly 1,200 feet long	kept Colorado River from flooding, generates enough energy each year to power 500,000 homes

It's Space Travel

It's one thing to build something impressive on Earth. It's another to build something out of this world! In 1957, the Soviets launched the first artificial satellite. Sputnik was the first man-made object to orbit Earth.

Since then, engineers have been working hard. They have sent people to the moon. They made space shuttles and the International Space Station. Today, they are sending probes to distant planets. An amazing telescope takes pictures of the universe. Engineers are even figuring out how to send people to Mars!

Reaching New Heights

The International Space Station (ISS) is a feat of cooperation. Countries around the world worked together to build a place for astronauts to live and study in space. The project took over 20 years and over $35 billion to complete.

Disaster in the Sky

With so many amazing feats, we can forget the cost of space travel. It isn't easy to send people into space. Equipment fails. Sometimes, people even die. One of the saddest days in space travel happened on January 28, 1986. Within 73 seconds into its flight, the space shuttle *Challenger* broke apart. All seven members of the crew were killed, including the first schoolteacher to travel into space.

Sinking Islands

Off the coast of Dubai lie 300 man-made islands. Arranged to look like a map, the islands are known as The World. At one time, they were a feat of engineering. Today, they can only be called a failure. The islands were designed to become luxury homes and resorts. Millionaires were invited to buy islands named after countries.

When they were first built, sand in the Gulf of Oman was moved to build the islands. Today, the islands are sinking into the sea. The builders didn't expect the islands to **erode**. The sand is sliding into the sea. The islands are disappearing. Despite this failure, plans are being made to build a new set of islands. They will be called The Universe.

one of The World's islands

The Engineer's Method

Modern engineers may be asked to solve a wide variety of problems. But whatever the problem, they follow similar steps to find a solution.

Analyze the problem. Is there a way to simplify the problem?

Study how other people have tried to solve the problem.

Design a possible solution.

Does it work as expected? Is it efficient?

Try a new solution. Study the results to reach a final product.

Share the results with the world.

Modern Mistakes

Engineers must work carefully to avoid errors in their calculations that could lead to tragedy, even death. Modern engineers study designs that led to disaster in the past. They learn what not to do. And they focus on making new designs that won't lead to failure.

13%
forget or make errors

The Swiss Federal Institute of Technology conducted a study about engineering disasters. They studied 800 cases in which someone had been killed. The data in this chart explains the ways an engineer can be at fault.

14%
are careless

16%
underestimate the ways their products might be used

1%
don't understand their
responsibilities

9%
rely on others
to make
decisions

7%
don't test the
product in a
new situation

1%
use poor
quality
materials

3%
other

36%
don't have enough
knowledge

Next Steps

The word *engineer* first appeared in the 1300s. That was when large military machines were used. Back then, it referred to things like **catapults** that could throw objects hundreds of feet. But the idea of engineering has been around much longer. Early humans used levers to lift heavy objects. Then, they learned to use pulleys to drag things. Soon, there were wheels. Armed with simple tools, early engineers created Stonehenge. They built the Great Pyramid. As they learned more, they built more. Today, engineers can send people into space. And they keep learning. What will they make next?

"To the optimist, the glass is half full. To the pessimist, the glass is half empty. To the engineer, the glass is twice as big as it needs to be."

—Unknown

Ups and Downs

In the Stone Age, an engineer's tools were simple. They had limited resources. These days, the world is full of possibilities. Our advanced technology gives engineers the chance to build more complex things. Look at the time line below to follow our progress. Imagine future engineering feats and failures that await us.

2950 BC
Stone Age engineers begin work on Stonehenge.

206 BC
Sections of the Great Wall of China are connected, creating one long wall.

AD 1912
The *Titanic* strikes an iceberg and sinks.

STOP! THINK...

- What tools did people have when they made these advances?

- How many people worked together?

- If you were going to create a massive project, what would you build?

AD 1937
The *Hindenburg* crashes.

AD 1998
The International Space Station brings together engineers from around the world.

AD 1969
The first human sets foot on the moon.

Glossary

blimp—a type of airship without an internal struction

canal—a waterway dug by people to let ships pass through

catapults—an ancient device used to throw weapons at enemies

computer-aided engineering (CAE)—computer programs that allow engineers to predict how their designs will work

conquered—defeated by force

dam—a wall that blocks a river

engineers—people who use math and science to build things

erode—to wear away by wind or water

explosives—things that are designed to explode

feats—great accomplishments

flammable—something that burns easily

Great Depression—the economic crisis and period of low business activity, beginning with the stock market crash in 1929 and continuing through most of the 1930s

helium—a gas used to float airships safely

hydrogen—a flammable gas

Industrial Revolution—a time when many machines were first being invented and used

molasses—a thick, sticky liquid made when processing sugar

passes—openings in a wall

pharaoh—an Egyptian king

segments—parts into which a thing is divided

signal towers—military command posts where soldiers stand watch to look for danger

Soviets—people, especially military leaders, of the former Union of Soviet Socialist Republics

spillways—places where extra water can run over or around a dam

steam shovels—machines used for digging

transcontinental—going across a continent

wages—payment for work

Index

Bibliography

Ames, Lee J. *Draw 50 Buildings and Other Structures: The Step-by-Step Way to Draw Castles and Cathedrals, Skyscrapers and Bridges, and So Much More.* **Watson-Guptill, 1991.**

This book is a simple guide to drawing buildings, bridges, and more. From the Eiffel Tower to the Taj Mahal, 50 man-made and natural structures are included.

Ash, Russell. *Great Wonders of the World.* **DK Children, 2006.**

This book includes not only the Seven Ancient Wonders but also many modern marvels. It includes photographs, illustrations, and explanations of these great wonders.

Birdseye, Tom. *A Kids' Guide to Building Forts.* **Roberts Rinehart, 1993.**

This book includes a brief history of forts and directions for building safe forts inside or outside, whether at the beach or in the snow.

Macaulay, David. *Built To Last.* **Houghton Mifflin Harcourt Publishing, 2010.**

Discover the how and why behind some of the world's most amazing structures ever created. This book brings to life castles, cathedrals, and other fascinating structures.

Herweck, Don. *All About Mechanical Engineering.* **Teacher Created Materials, 2008.**

Learn about the basic principles of engineering, including force, acceleration and deceleration, action, and reactions. Find out how engineers use these concepts to make our lives easier.

More to Explore

Encyclopedia Titanica
http://www.encyclopedia-titanica.org

This website is a very thorough collection of information regarding the *Titanic*. Learn more about the ship design, people, history, and more all in one place.

Greatest Engineering Achievements of the 20th Century
http://www.greatachievements.org/

This website includes a detailed time line and categorized achievements from the 20th century.

How Stuff Works: Engineering
http://science.howstuffworks.com/engineering-channel.htm

This website covers information on highways, subways, railways, and bridges.

Top 10 Worst Engineering Disasters
http://listverse.com/2007/12/04/top-10-worst-engineering-disasters

This website has a photograph and summary of 10 disasters including the Cleveland East Ohio Gas Explosion, the St. Francis Dam Flooding, and the Boston Molasses Disaster.

Seven Wonders of the Ancient World
http://www.unmuseum.org/wonders.htm

At this website, each of the Seven Wonders of the Ancient World has its own section that includes detailed descriptions and images, as well as information on how they might have been constructed.

About the Author

Stephanie Paris is a seventh generation Californian. She has her Bachelor of Arts in psychology from the University of California, Santa Cruz and her multiple-subject teaching credential from California State University, San Jose. She has been an elementary classroom teacher, an elementary school computer and technology teacher, a homeschooling mother, an educational activist, an educational author, a web designer, a blogger, and a Girl Scout Leader. She loves using the tools of engineering to solve everyday problems. She currently lives in Germany with her husband and children.